LOVE IS FOREVER

ON THIS EARTH AND IN ANY OTHER

Love Is Forever

On this Earth and in Any Other

CECILIA HELENA AMAYA

SilverWood

Published in paperback by SilverWood Books 2012
www.silverwoodbooks.co.uk

For the purposes of authenticity the poems in this book have been published exactly
as the author intended, with no correction other than a light proofread.

ISBN 978-1-78132-033-4

British Library Cataloguing in Publication Data
A CIP catalogue record for this book is available from the British Library

Set in Bembo by SilverWood Books
Printed on paper sourced responsibly

Contents

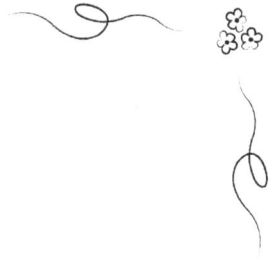

Love is for Ever and Ever

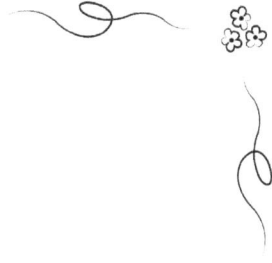

Summer Day

The sun is out
a smell of green
a taste of youth
around the earth
and birds fly across the world
yet singing to the blue
yet challenging the winds.

Sun and birds
and green and heat
– You all at once –
out of my reach
stay the same
'till I come back.

Morning of fresh water drops
I want to say hello
to my love.
Days of sun,
I wish you would forever last.

Please Think to Celebrate

Please think to celebrate
our meeting a year ago.
You forgot the date
I did *NOT*
but anyway…
haven't I known you
from other lives before?
I feel at home this is my fate
for longer than a life-time.
But still there is a lot to say,
I rather say good bye
for now, at last
'till you come again,
always.

If Far Away

If far away
there was no soul
to penetrate your soul.

If the wind
whistles high now
and the rain gets you cold.

Knock this door
now at once
someone inside
is dying – waiting
and that arms
are ready to welcome
you back.

I Wish

I wish...
You were *here* and *now*
both laying down
in this carpet
cushions under the heads
looking at the rain
starting now to fall
your arms where they belong
your leg across myself
as it used to be
I wish, my love, and wish.

Hurry Up Life

Hurry up, life!!
I am fed up
of standing by
while in some lighter corner
the laughter sounds
hurry up, or have me at once;
from only two chokes
if I'm to choose
and stick to no one
and as if, as how I feel
and if I'm kind
I sat, let me stay
now in between
always.

You Simply Stay

Sit in silence, like I am doing,
no words, no sounds,
no whispers even...
and slow down your movements
for I have gone
inside my mind;
for I have withdrawn
myself from this world;
but don't go away:
you simply stay
for I might like
to stretch my arm
and find you close;
so please remain
in case my soul
dares to look for your soul;
just in case my mind
does not enjoy
to feel alone.
So don't go away
if I close my eyes,
if I don't say a word:
you simply stay.

I Have Loved You

I have loved you
in the sun
when flowers and leaves
have an orgy of green.

I have loved you
in the snow
when the white
becomes the god
and in piles of white mud
we dug our feet
and walked along.

I have loved you
by the sea
when the waves
come and go,
when a promise to return
is written forever
in the sand.

I have loved you
with your friends
with the gayness of fair youth,
with the nonsense of a child
yet enjoying not to age
and reluctant to grow up.

I have loved you
in your chats;
transient words;
replying echoes;
soundless crowds.

I have loved you
in your dreams
being god/being great
being simply a "HUMAN BEING".

I have loved you
you at once
you in the future,
you in the past.
Let me hold you in my arms.
Let me love you with my mind
you, ALONE,
you and I.

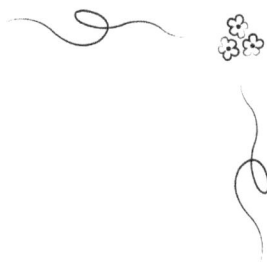

Today's Pain

Today's despair
tomorrow's songs
blown to the air
by someone else.

Secrets exposed
to passing souls;
you must learn the message
and never repeat.

A question still hanging;
an answer never heard:
are yesterday's dreams
today's pain?

What is Your Name?

What is your name…
I ask myself once a day.

Who are you who comes to create
confusion in this categorical silence of mine.
Who are you… I did not expect anyone.

And often I wonder and think of the beginning.
I did not expect you
for plans I had, many plans
of leaving at last
leaving forever
still leaving, however…
any departure now is no longer harmless.

And I was sure of nothing
but of my very own unattachment.

The end would not matter;
any ending worthy would be
but never again would I rot while there is still some
breath left.

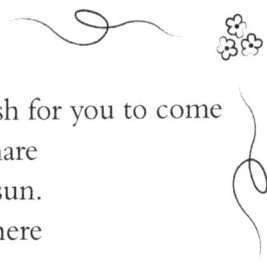

And then you appeared… I did not wish for you to come
I have forgot how to share
just for myself was the sun.
But you already were there
and I looked for no one.
You know now
I never suspected your existence
who are you who cast some doubt in my only certainty.

What madness unknown-for-me is that
of mentally sharing
bits of a whole
that ever was so beyond
my aspiration.

Why do you build up on me
the wish for where I just come from
it was not that easy.
And if never before one dare approached a success
Where are you then for whom even to belong
completely
still seems too little.

I want your name as an argument in your favour
for I will accuse in front of the tribunal
of my individualism he to whom I wish
to give
even that nobody knows yet I possess.

Search

And all what I needed was silence,
an unbreakable silence, a quiet face;
for that I locked my door
and my windows I shut
and kept quiet myself,
but it did not work;
I still hear the yields,
and the echoes,
and the noise:
and all what I wanted was silence;
for that I tried to cover
the noise with my voice;
the yields with my prayers
and all that was in vain:
my voice had not the power;
my prayers were never heard
and all what I searched for was silence…
For that I left my home,
and left my brothers, as well;
for that I lose my faith
and came to be alone;
not to hear a word
and met only the people who could understand my
search;
who could even look for the same;
but after all I haven't found none
– no one at all –
who would put his arms
around myself

and say no words
for all what I needed was silence
and in silence I lost my god,
my faith,
my home,
my brothers – if one
but still I can clearly listen
echoes of what I once have heard.

Bits of Life

Wandering around like a child
who looks for the first reasons of life
I go through mine
gathering rays of sun,
gusts of wind
bits of love
from all
but no one
ever I have met that gives me more.

And to life
I have penned my soul;
and to people
dedicated my mind;
and for them once I cried
but I have seen not yet
whatever for.

And pieces of my heart
I have put together
to follow on my searching
but bits of love
is what I got...

And if when I start to speak aloud
bits of words
is what comes out
and bits of those
is what you receive
I wonder... then
if our eyes are not yet blind
or if it is just as well
this life of ours
bits of somebody else's life.

So, please! Let me
hang on my individuality
as the only possession of my own
for nothing else can be true
if, finally,
only bits of life is what we got.

You Look at Me

You look at me...
a question mark is in your eyes
you ought to know
why
I sit alone,
why I sit in silence
while the people play around?

I think, my dear;
shall I tell you what about.
Shall I tell you what's in my mind?

I look so static
but do not trust my quietness
for my link
with the world
is always on the move.

I think of food
but not for me.
I think of help
that I could give,
I think of loves
that I don't know
but could yet learn
and still I don't want to
or feel so scared
I think of kids
that were not born.

I think of money
with bread and honey
for boys and girls
and mothers and men
not yet too hungry to digest.

I think of the people
that have passed my sight
and I haven't seen;
they are now well gone
and no one I recall.

I think of the times
I felt happiness
and the millions of loves
that have said "goodbye".

I think "why I do not go
– no matter the place -
but always far away
to meet the one I don't know,
to hear what I many times have heard
miles beyond the sound
where the words seem estranged".

I think of the hours
of sixty empty long minutes
that have left life
and belong now to the memories
hideaway of cowards.

I think about drinks
not once for the world
but all them for me
for I do enjoy
drinking while I sit
in the yellow cushion of my silence
with a spell of liqueur around me
and marking a thick line
between your world and my world,
between your wish and my being;
between your need for possession
and my need to be free.
I think of a cold shower
unknown sex-experience
for the wise "all-said-all-tried" civilised European.

Time Over

Our love is old today
we made it age
too soon and fast...
for you were blind
with a fictitious image
of myself
that I never was
and intent not to be
for I could not change
to fit into your mind
with standards and patterns
with measures and clichés
with establishments and links
even though I have dreamed
even though I have tried.

No. I rather don't…
It is time to stop
and for it I would say
good bye to all
I need a friend
before than a love
I need to talk
but not to quarrel
and peace and silence
I must have
those days of tiredness
of misfit in society
from a life without end

of 24 hours of yields
and meaningless dialogues;
for I need companion
instead of an affair
in my endless nights
of ideas that fight
their way through my head
their life to mine's cost.
I come from a place
where peace is forbidden
where sincerity is a myth
I just left hell
for someone else called heavens
and I lost my faith
and my brothers I left
and I lost my god, my god as well
and said good bye to comfort
in days full of laziness
of climax of anxiety
of memories in black
but you would never understand
so I close my lips forever
on my very own past;
so I offer you a deal
the deal of friendship
my mind you may have for granted,
my soul full of sensitivity
with long talks and all the madness
the same way it used to be;

I offer you my kindness
my happiness is yet your asset
to listen and no talking

to give and not receive
I offer you my person
my individual own-self
without request
without demands
without limitations of time.

A Hint of Soul

And there she was:
darks skies, lights on land,
and a peculiar cold wind
as a sign.
There she was,
my aim – at last! –
five minutes away
that I could not count
for they seemed too long
and I was coming from a place
where time has been lost
for a century in my life,
for a life in the world.

And then I saw myself
getting off the plane,
putting feet on a land
ever since like mine,
ever after in my heart;
and today I ask the world
if ever before to this place I have come
or if – beyond any time –
here I was born
for there is something inside
that recalls the steps, the lights,
even the cloudy greys of my sky,
and a hint of soul
that still here remains…

Mercenary Love

Mercenary love,
ghost in the dark,
elusive ghost
flying with the wind,
bubbling desires
like autumn leaves,
fragile existence
of secret dreams,
eternal hours
searching the nights,
restrained emotions
without display
unfulfilled feelings,
forbidden fires
of dying flames.
one day not far,
Bohemian over,
still in silence,
I'll say farewell.
one night not distant
when dreams are over
I'll cry and cry.

All at Once

Between two unattainable worlds I struggle:
your life/his life
both at once!
keeping mine
in the amorphous darkness
of confusion
and transcendent thoughts
hand in hand
with a frivolous present,
of non-repeatable memories
of two unique loves;
and I am ONE
forever to no end
– the ageless swallow –
with extended wings
ready to leave
the forbidden shore
of indecisiveness and doubt,
who forgot to compromise
for bits or parts,
and yet would like
the two both
and at the same time,
to live and last
through evo's lasting turn;
to love and dig up
the minute of each mind
in endless nights
overwhelmed by

past;
present;
future
all at once,
You,
He,
and I.

Please REMAIN!

From the middle of my mind
I ask you, please REMAIN!

Let the world
go in circles;
or back and forth;
and up and down,
and move with it
the moving phase
of your mentality;
and build and change
– or yet destroy –
what has been set
but indeed
stop men from going ahead;
the evil for man's sake;
but, then, beyond the dust,
in spite of the rain;
of the left and red
right and black
may the you in you
forever REMAIN
Until I move away
– or longer after me –
for I could not look at your face
and see the self in you
no longer is there…
that forgot to REMAIN.

Some Mountains as the End

Some mountains as the end and only hope.
Not just as those so close, too high
that once the sun have faded
and stop the air for my breath;
although the same.
and if one time
they rarefied my atmosphere,
today, they are only the frame
of the cold of a cold city,
with cold inhabitants, no soul.
The impotent blindness of he
who would like to see
beyond but cannot
for his wish is continuously obstructed
by amorphous walls of wasted land,
of acres of loneliness
partner of human rats –
imperative and unique fruit
of being who despite their
never were joined in an only cause
and whose non-classifiable passions
surpass the Good and Bad.

continued

The continuous 'trick-track'
of an electric artefact
– made abroad –
is my closest neighbour;
the same machine should be hit
with a vigour proper of a youth alive
yet too soft to follow a rhythm
and sufficiently hard to exceed the noise
and white sheets full of adjacent words
should perform a thought,
an idea; perhaps a concept;
but alien, always alien
as are the hours of this day
followed and re-followed
by other days, more days…
all alien, of course,
as these mountains
and those flat fields
which are only a pretension of horizon
and desert their ambition
at the first contact
with a pile of mud
to resign themselves
to be just a geometric angle.

Alien is my country:
paradoxical sequence
expressed from a lonely and desolated soul;
colourful visions
that, by the right of nature,
portrait the hands
of he, who so many times,
has digged up its flesh
the extract the food yet wet
with tears and blackened by the swear
of misused strength
without even a deserved occasion for cleanliness.

A Minute

A minute of you I pray
let me have
close your eyes,
come to me:
life is short and has a face
which I like.

No tomorrow is in my mind
no past is left that I can see
is you and me;
your wish/my wish
one thought in both
if there is one;
for life is short,
for we are young
and superficiality
is our god.
so close your eyes
to other lives
that only see
what is outside
and come to me.

Tomorrow we'll die
and in empty graves
will be buried
these precious bodies of ours
with minds that fit
in no place at all
for can not trust
what faith has lost;
for can't say 'Yes' to what is 'No'
with souls
that will wander
from there on.

So let's make love
a minute of 24 hours
for life is short
and has a face that I enjoy.

Alien is My City

Alien is my city
forbidden site
for he, who mad
with his own anguish,
looks to drown it
inside the horrible noise
of repaired mechanisms
and furious horns
onomatopoeic sounds
of unpronounceable words
yet too many times been said
disturbing thus men
who – for their misfortune –
still have faith.

Alien is the public park;
witty laugh of an elite
keeping for itself even the green
in private fields,
sliced off the body of static buildings,
faithful copy of many others
risen up in other parts
vain long years ago,
and repeated here
as many times as the miserable
could swear and re-swear of his fate.

Alien is my country.
my scenery; my parks and my cities.
alien is my life
in its 15 hours of light
price set up on my impotent baby body
with my need to eat for witness.

Today I feel the hands of the clock
as knives in my flesh,
in the insides
of this my feverish wish
of living;
of thinking;
of owning!,
The 12 noon that set my mental freedom
seems unachievable, remote and profaned.

Must I submit
and give in my capacity of thoughts;
must I fight and hide
my true wish of running away!;
never was a place for me rated
if my very own country is an alien.

Green on the Land

Green on the land,
blue on the sky
and in between a milliard
of other colours
and other lights
of clothes of young people
of peaceful guys
who long for sincerity
and have joined the life
and feel not ashamed
of their wishes' shade;
people like you and me,
like us
gathered as one
to listen to the band
this bright afternoon
of early autumn
laying on yellowish leaves
as if they were soft cushions.

I look around
I look through the crowd
to find your eyes
for you should be
with me / with us
sitting on the grass
to cry of laugh
legs crossed
in a yoga position
touching your neighbour's arms
and breathing an air
saturated of sound.

I look around
but you are not among my crowd.

I search for you
with any scarf
around your neck,
your face alive letting out the feeling
the sound might arise.

I see the crowd
I am among
and hear the sound
but not your voice
and see the colours we used to love
I am alone
and feel you ought to be
besides my side
but you are not.

Thank You

Thank you for being alive
just like that…
For being as you are
and letting me be
the way I am.

Thank you, my dearest bourgeoisie,
for fighting against social injustice
as if you would agree
with socialist's minds –
do not say you don't,
for I do know;
do not deny
is written in your eyes,
for it is you I trust.

Thank you for believing
without enquiries;
for accepting me as I come.

Thank you, great men,
for being the greatest one;
for being conservative
and letting me be
the liberal wild
fighting to survive
in a world doomed to die.

Thank you for letting me find
my own way to the surface,
to reach and touch the light;
for keeping your god to yourself
many thanks,
even though mine I have lost
despite my searching for no other one
for what I have seen in your being
supplies the need of belief
in a utopian dream,
and keep my feet attached to the earth
for you have a miraculous power
of recalling what I want
and tears could never come
when my eyes are full of life;
no room for thieves of joy;
no time for resignation
of another life after dying
for I do have quite enough
with the one I have got
and the day I say "good bye",
I would say it to all
but for myself I will keep these words:
"thank you, for being as you are,
for being alive".

Half of Myself

A morning in blue
with sky full of clouds
that move
just like you
and you and I
or I and you
for both of you
are just like one:
if I stay
and if you go
will still be the same
or if I walk away
and you remain
what is will be,
what was has come
a long way from the past
and still will last.
For we do not age
for we don't have time
for we have not found
our place in the world
for we don't compromise
for pieces and halves
and yet give all
but expect less than none.

Today that you are gone
to see other blues in the sky
I notice an empty space
around my side
but feel as well
that you have left
but half of myself
is on your way.

Myth

Help!
I created a myth
and today
I am a victim of it.

Help!
– come and break the illusion,
find my being;
give a scream
(but not too loud).

Help!
I built up a legend on my life.
Help, for he is too scared of the myth that I am.
– come and discover the secret;
for I am getting tired;
for I am getting restless;
for I am getting sad.
of being the ideal
I grew fed up
and just for once
I wanted to be real!

Help!
… but don't give a scream
… don't shake my being…
… don't break my dreams…
for all that has been done
and it proved vain.

Help!
– I am a myth,
and he is too scared.
I am a myth which has been built up
through the days
through the nights
and now weeps to wake up.

I am a myth
with an inner being
that longs to be real;
but he is too scared
and I am growing weak;
is nothing left for me to do,
but him,
he should not hesitate…
for the myth in me
is nothing else
but my very own self
with a new conception of the world,
with new ideas for my life.
So
mystery;
or dream;
or soul;
or world:

The myth is me, myself or I;
he should not be so scared,
I have touched life with both my hands.

Summer's Illness

Floating in the air
are my thoughts,
and the window
shall remain unclosed;
and the curtain
will not so fixate
the freshness
longing to walk in;
and the sun
shall distort its lights;
and the wind
is to move them fast.
Don't move the scene
in front of me
when I fall to sleep.
I want the sun
to wake me up;
I want the breeze
to touch my flesh
and all at once
when opening my eyes
shall sing:
the day is up
I haven't died
during the night.

Take Care, Pity Me

Please care, pity me...
is all you hear
and give yourself, your only-own-self
and they will still say

I have seen the world
with opened doors
to pelerines or friends;
to wanderers or loves;
for I have believed one time
but lost my faith in the way
for I have trust,
trust, as well
but... care
− I just can't care anymore.
for I gave away
all what I was
and potential being as a tip;
for I have receive
bits of nothing
lots of bits
and I don't care.

continued

Pity for the boys
who have lost their parents
but I don't believe in families;
pity for the girls who will never marry
but I don't believe in weddings:
pity for the grown ups…
no. I just don't care.
I pity NO ONE
I take and give
and still I think
I could do more
but I don't care.

And people play
the game of life
but don't know what
it is like
and people dream
of giving and receiving
but I pity no one
and I could care less
and I will not pat
nobody's head
of backs of grown ups
I just don't care.

And if people start to think
that I am in a shell
of protective self-defence
I will say, yes indeed,
I have built up a fence
to hide the ashes not yet black
of my days of broken heart
but never I have asked
please do care.

Pagan Minutes

You are giving me
what I expect from someone else;
and I give him
what you are longing to receive.

I wonder where
– through walking in the dark –
these lives of ours
have got mixed up.

I wonder why
you look at me
with loving eyes
full of a desire
that I don't find
in whom I look.

And I give you none
of what you are giving me;
and yet I receive lots
of what I don't need,
but from him…
I just don't know.

I believe up in some place
– in the highest of nothingness –
must exist an evil power
playing around with our souls;
but I don't enjoy the game,

and you – for sure – feel the same;
and he, my beloved friend,
is dreaming of someone
who has lost
bit by bit the hope,
the faith
while he – the player –
has an orgy with your love,
his dreams,
my tears
running already for too many years
and prolonged from the past,
which have come back together
to join the new ones just born:
from your vain love
his scariness;
my faith lost
and a game:
the game of god!
So you or she
or he and I:
must we play the role
or just say "no"
and then make love
for an eternity in god's minds
you, he and I
or we – the same;
for all of us
are played like puppets
and I don't like
the taste of such a game.

Long Rain

For three long days
the rain has fallen down;
my city is wet
its heart is cold.
I wonder if it weeps
for I would want
to weep myself.

I wonder if the grey
which has faded the sun
is not just the shadow
of my pain;
for it used to be clear
for it used to be blue
some time before now.

I wonder where and when
I ran too weak
and dripped a tear
in some lonely street
for I know well
they grow as seeds;
they fall as rain
and the rain has fallen
for three days.

I want to know
where I've lost it
to pick it up
and put it back
to where it belongs,
and no one would complain
or moan of an innocent rain
which is only my fault:

The projection of a love
that has vanished
that is dead;
for that I weep…
for it, it rains…

Digging Too Deep

Digging too deep to find the base;
climbing too high
to search for light,
the truth, the justice
I lost myself.
I can't go back;
I use my mind
to seek a line
and follow it
for quite sometime,
but find at the end
that the line goes dead
and I am lost again.

I follow the people
who once tried to smile,
I smile back to them
but after a while
I discover
our ways are not the same.

I use my body to find the real
I feel the cold in my hands,
I froze my arms
and let my feet bare
or try to stop my existence,
it is all in vain
I am lost myself:
the end is not even near.

I don't know where to look at
I am giving up…
I seeked inside,
I checked outside;
I climbed high
I gave myself to all
and lost my way in the search.

I wonder, though
where have I blundered
for all I wanted
was peace and love
and social justice.

One Flash of Countless Lights/The Evo

A day; two nights.
A kiss; a song.
A prayer/a curse.
The wind just gone,
or just the idea
not yet quite born;
the whisper of a word,
yet the sound of the world.

One here; the other far apart:
or both at once.
The place is heavens;
the site is lost
in the middle of our minds,
in the depth of our lust.

Going to, or coming back
from labyrinth to crucible:
the you in you
my I, inside
with one smile
that fades the sun
and colours the black
of one and thousand
or a million and one
wishes of mine;
no unity of time.
No age to count
– what was has been

ever since the world began –
with days and nights
of milliard of minutes each one
in the evo of our brains
doomed to be washed of any end,
of any limit of time
in two beings saturated of feelings
or one single flash of countless lights.

New Year's Eve

And they all repeated at once:
Happy New Year;
impersonal echo
from a faceless crowd.
I looked around
for truthful eyes
to share my soul
too big for me that night,
and found the answer
in the glass window
repeating my image,
reflecting my voice,
and hidden legs
under an expensive dress
confirmed themselves
as my only friends
who could read my anguish,
but they were shaking then:
I drank too much
to celebrate
a Happy New Year
with an empty glass.

Religious Carnival

Gamin, little gamin
walking barefoot in cold streets
let me have a dream
of you approaching me
to sing my song that I composed
for you and the world.

Sit here on the grass
– green brown leaves –
that are not your;
that are not mine
for you own nothing,
and I left all
a New Year's Eve
when I realised
the colourful crystal
were not for you/neither for me,
and two transparent tears
fell to wet the land
and grew up as flowers in my mind.

But close your eyes
and let the light
go faded by it
for they are little pearls in black
that shine and grin,
that create shadows, if you want.

Stretch your hands
and leave your fingers free
not to catch of grab
a change of food,
but to caress a world
created for you
and that belongs to none of us.

Gamin, little gamin,
who runs barefoot
to get nowhere,
to meet no one,
stay with me this New Year's Eve
and sing my song
that for a year
has been inside my soul
but yet was never born
for you were there
and I have gone
beneath your sun;
little face darkened by the dust;
big brown eyes
staring at a chance
of grabbing someone's watch
learning too fast
to smell the law
and punching wheels
of red and black cards
with ladies inside

who pass along
to be charitable in some other's land
and disgusted
at your muddy face
feel pity
but keep their bags safe.

Gamin, little gamin,
I have seen your face
in some other place
across the miles;
I think of you
this New Year's Day
and to you I life my cup
and soak a question in my champagne:

Where did they hide you
when the Pope came
who provided the bed and bread
– soft touch –
first time in your life
who fed you then
during those profitable days
of religious carnival?

Bohemia I Am

Like any Bohemia
I go around the world
joining bits and lots
and drunk by sips of life;
I stay or depart
and I go back and forth
but tie myself to no one.

I cross the seas
of the unknown,
and climb the hills
to see beyond,
to plan new trips,
to set new goals.
I sit and watch
and feel quite deep.
I drink and think:
that's all I know;
that's all I want;
for I can not
tie myself to a dream
for all the dreams are in my fate
and soon I have to leave
and go away
beyond the nights,
along the days.

I could never stop
– not that again –

for once I did
and lost myself,
and the bohemia in me
at once was born;
ever since I know
the beginning of a dream
sets the time for me to leave;
and if ever I hear a sweet call
– from one of the thousand roads-
and it does claim for my presence,
I shut my eyes;
I cover my ears
and the bohemia says: red lights,
departure/danger.

I move again
killing dreams not yet born
rather than dying old ones
saying too soon no
to what I haven't thought of;
but there is a bohemia inside
who drinks, who thinks;
who laughs sometimes;
who goes beyond the words,
behind the sounds,
and loves, *even that*!
But says "good bye".

The Bug of Love

Because love finishes
the individual in the person;
because love alienates the soul,
and teaches to fear;
because love ends
any sort of belief
and spoils the pleasure
of just one being
in front of the rest,
in the middle of the world;
for love imitates
the visibility scope,
and deteriorates
the vision itself
you will find one not too clear day
you see not beyond your love
and breath in, rather than out;
for love destroys the faith
when one – at last! –
has decided to trust;
for love brings tears
and bitter taste
to eyes not shining yet
and lips framed with lines
will have deeper grieves:
for love is cruel;
for love is fool;
for love is a myth
that minimizes any sense of the real

and blindfolds your mind,
today,
my beloved friend,
that your face is cold
and your hands extrange
I ask life
for love's sake –
let's make love
before it grows dark,
before it is too late!

Like Anyone Else Does

While me,
with my innermost sensible being,
found no more ways
to say NO
and forgot the meaning of YES,

You,
with your practicality
and based on years of fullness
did not recall the taste
of the beginning
in a soul moistened
with the wetness of crossing feelings,
of grasping life
always with two hands.

I ask tonight,
if there ever was a sense
of unselfish appreciation,
or if it is just
your own pride
overtaking your sincere side
and playing games
like anyone else does…

Coming From the Unknown

Intangible,
like any ray of sun;
like a wave
in the middle of the sea
touching no shore
in a measured time,
in an ever-returning scope.

Unreachable,
like the goal never set
for all misfortune and happiness
I am:
imprecise;
remorse;
ambivalent;
the impossible dream
of all dream and mind,
and the untouchable hand
of a friend who died,
for my misery
I am;
and I wish to stay
whenever I depart;
and I want to cry
but instead I smile
with my intangible nature
of colours too light
and shadows too dark,
setting me a place

in no man's land;
and yet I would like to give
the part of me
that tastes sweet
when you approach my being;
but an inner-bit
is due to be alone
– don't break the rule –
for doing so
you tear off
pieces of a soul
which would wonder ever since
to set new bonds
and establish new links
between a man
and an unknown world
of years ahead
(or years ago,
which man has forgot
and history does not explain)
when I could be myself
and still be your love
without the limiting space
of just two souls
and the cold,
self-defensive look of doubt;
no one around to fix me a place
– pre-established/organized –
to come or go

whenever I please
to prove the fullness of my being
being itself;
returning to you
and loving your innermost
with my frenzied youth
– never doomed to age –
when after some time
the dust turns strange
and the wind whistles
high notes.

When Yes Means *No*

To be your love
and yet be myself,
keeping my life in the same shell
of the unknown;

To love you to the end
in ecstasies of frenzied youth
still saying yes and no
to my going/returning
to embrace the soul
of bodies with no face
for I need the unknown
as the plants need a seed
to become trees
yet saying goodbye
to all dreams
of dreamers' brains
knowing well
the no means yes
and the laugh is mere tears
in an absurd world
of windows closed.

What Price Oh Life!

I search for a man
who takes me as I am;
sweet/strong being
yet too weak
whenever winter comes.
I look for a man who remains besides me
wherever I go;
who sees me to leave
yet saying, so long...
and open doors
will always be
for me,
for my song,
for my going.

I look for someone
who stays
but never lasts
to the spleen
in bored souls.

I look for one
who teaches me to love
by letting me love him
in the gardens of my mind.
I look for him
who has been lost
in love's eternity:
what price, oh life!

Beings of the Sun

In the fire of our eyes we met.
Crossing roads led on to us;
falling bridges support our beings;
defeated gods behold our beliefs
and sunsets open the light into the day
and sunrises close the dark of the world
and I say hello with tears yet to run,
and I say goodbye smile after smile
for we are beings of the sun
, and dig our feet in white snow
and link our hands in piles of white mud
to prove the gold of golden backs
is hot, is love, is real, is fact,
the highest of the heights,
and test the hell of each one's hell,
and we pray to the life of deads
and sing with the wind
the whistling song of windows opened
and fly with it
the fragile thoughts we build,
the rumours we heard beyond the sea
and leave our hair flying
and fly our minds
to meet the crowd
in the desert line
between night and day,
between life and dead:
beings of the sun we are.

No Return

Someone has seen;
someone has come;
someone is gone;
someone is gone;
someone has said.
but we have though:
come along with me,
my beloved being,
we are moving ahead
to where no brain has been,
from where there is no return.

Lovers of the Sun

We are lovers
of the sun;
lovers of the day we are;
and love loving
for love's sake
and lose balance is a love is lost;
if a face has vanished or fades away.

We are lovers
of the night;
loving love
to the climax of the dark;
and play the day
without hands
and fade the light with our eyes.

We are lovers
of the time
counting nights
and counting hours
by the unity of our lust;
by the distance
between our brains
stopping always wherever we go;
starting over
whenever we come.

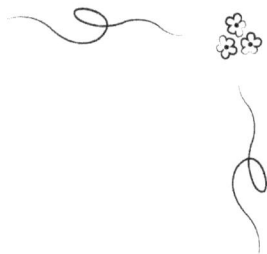

We are lovers
of the sea;
in forbidden shores
we always meet;
in unknown waters
we become gods
beings of the wind…

And love lead us
from nowhere to the end
no love is left
that we have not felt;
no tear has ever fell
that we haven't shed
and we pray to life
and we sing to death:
for we conquered it
we are the kings of the earth.

The Meaningless Goodbye

Then we ask ourselves
what have we done to deserve
a negative face
in an unattainable world.

Then we come to claim
the reason for being alone
in a crowded pace.

Then we cry
– a tearless sob is ours –
but smile to other people
and show cynicism
as a protective mask.

Then we want to die
and give up all
for there is no hope;
for there is no laugh...

But we indeed forgot
that day we, as lions,
with an expressionless face have said
no… maybe… perhaps…
and played along
the game of prolonging agonies
'till finally we pronounced
a meaningless goodbye
that meaningfully came true
for we were yet to compromise to realize
it was life this time
who was passing by
but now it is too late:
the chance is gone…

Match

A colour that is not
the colour in my mind;
a shape that is not
the shape I have touched;
a voice not matching
the sweet I once heard
rising up a milliard bells
to call for an orgy of sounds
when the lights dare to fade;
a hair that is not the long
– the wild hair I have loved –
when walking through the wind
the forms forget their place
and call to be rebuilt
and when looking at the sun
the shades become in fire.
I was alone,
but I know someone
who has the size of my desire.
my unique ambition is achieved
when I caress his brain with my brain;
and I say hello
kissing his lips
and I say good night
kissing his arms
to go deep into my dreams
with my ambiguous grin
and peaceful eyes:

I have seen
what no one has ever seen;
I have felt the climax
of two beings
being matched;
I have met someone
who has the size of my desire.

Substitution

I, alone,
for I changed the brown of some warm arms
for an electric blanket not yet plugged,
and the life of some eyes for a faceless crowd,
and I said goodbye to my love
with an empty exile,
masquerade of my anguish;
for I subsisted his presence
for a book and a pencil
and an avant-garde newspaper
to kid myself, to carry on
'till I find again my way to him/his world;
a microworld of two
where the horizon goes beyond the time of times
when he says yes to my uninhibited love
and I say no
to his demanding please stay;
a macrocosmos of we both
if he smiles
and I kiss his soul with my soul.
I am alone
but I let the image of my own
in the mirror of a room
where he looks at his face everyday.

Is Sold Out My Return

White fields hitting my sight
as forgetting any sins
from unknown lives
and erasing any anguish in compromised beings,
let me write my name
in your fresh whiteness
for I want to last
'til the sun comes up
and I want to feel the melting
in myself,
for I am to leave this winter night
and go to a place in the unknown
where I have been
ever since I was born.

White flakes of microduration,
be the echoes of my words
singing to the world
my transient song
for passing things are we both,
you on the fields,
I on my soul,
and I am afraid
I overheard a whisper in the snow:
time comes,
time goes,
Yesterday I came
is sold out my return.

Some More Time

There is nothing else but life
and life is so close to death
lift your hand
and open your eyes
and touch the flower of time
for lips moistened by feelings
will project in the heights
some ideas of some brains,
while you, the human, will claim
to the gods
life is here, life is short
some more time, some more time.

The Skill of Wisdom

A ray of sun
coming through a whole
in grotty walls
– distorted light in a site
never before exposed
to the experience of the warmth
and the shadows giving room
to a wider silver gloom
– gentle touch of someone's hand –
reaching souls from the outside
linking dreams
of transient beings
– restless dreamers of no land –
who are cold,
who are made;
who have gone inside their shells
and will never come again.
– Wise they are!

Breaking Away

Breaking away?
– you must be brave.
Going far?
– you must have luck,
and the dress
you are to wear;
and the hat;
and the plane
you have to catch:
You are brave
to leave your maid;
you have luck;
a soul of ice
and no heart.

And somewhere beyond the seas
someone's heart no longer in one piece;
somewhere no one recalls
there is a mind
that has been behold
to the unknown/to the past.

If it was too late to run away.
They won it back
when maliciously remarked:
'you are going far'
'you are too brave'
and a golden tear
dripped in silence/and disappeared:
Everything at once was said.

Empty Space

Empty space surrounds my life…
like the silence in a lonesome night;
is it the feeling of non-said prayers?
Or the voice of someone gone
who forgot to say goodbye?

Empty space fills up my room
with the cold of wasted youth,
with the dreams of alien lands;

Empty space around my side
– I am alone –
or I am with someone
I still feel the shivering absence
of the sun.

Empty space, empty life
when I go/when I come.
When I love…
when I dislike…
or both at once
There is an empty place
around my side
that I forgot to fill soon enough.

HELP

At the edge of a precipice
I wish
a miraculous thing would happen
but it doesn't.
Just a bit more
and it will be too late;
hurry up, oh life,
let it be the hint of a dream
I once had
let me smile again.

Hurry up, voice I heard,
break the silence of my night
locked inside
long enough
for I would not dare come out on my own
I need your hand.

Hurry, oh sun,
and light another day,
perhaps today
I may hear the magic phrase
for which I wait,
for what I long.

New Creed

Hints of doubt
reaching my mind,
transient bits of sound
that break at touch
yet remaining
after the sun is gone.

Intangible sentences escaped
from odd communications
– distorted reflections –
a word once missed,
a voice yet heard,
and a telephone call
linking a memory now sleeping
yet awakening old wishes.

Uncertainty in bits,
and the assurance of knowing
contentedness is beyond my reach,
that he passed my sight
and did not call him.

Doubts, painful knives
fragile like the wind,
transient clouds
knowing well to be wrong
still asking why
and unwilling to repeat
doomed to fail:
and to accept it
as a creed!

If I Were

If I were to say goodbye
I would say it with a smile,
perfect mark
for crossing feelings
to be hidden
yet expressed.

If I were to leave my place
− cosy corner in your arms −
I would let the touch of hands
overtake
painful memories from the past.

If I were to call you again,
I would life my cup and say:
"You who saw beyond my being";
"You who linked
one brain to a brain";
"You who felt the sun of suns
and is wild/but has cried..."

If I were to write my name,
I would carve:
I lived my life,
and I failed,
BUT I TRIED!

Human Geometry

Schemes in the air,
gusts of wind moving them;
empty space
to separate
forms and shapes;
vicious cycle
with no end
reaching the top,
yet falling low,
drawing the curve
of destiny in full,
setting the line
of no return
but the low and high
joint-venture
of movement and repetition;
distant gap
to determine
the value
in degrees
of man despair;
the net figure
of a triangle
with human angles
for the game.

Marching Feet

Drawing lines in the sky,
setting goals,
crossing road
for crossing lives,
saying yes,
saying no,
saying good bye
when passing by
and carrying on
to some place
not yet known,
to no where
to no land;
still the same
still the old
for doomed to walk
are we all
and bound to pass
and go ahead...:
I have reached my end
and found no one;
I have walked straight
and heard no sound
but the walking steps
of someone behind
marching feet,
moving legs,
hanging arms
which forgot

to close around someone,
naked forms,
they have gone;
transient shapes,
they have passed;
open your arms
to embrace the next…

In Vain

Words to the air;
opened mouths
to proclaim
with new sounds
new hope, new faith;
but they don't know
all that was said
sometime before
they were born;
someone else's worlds;
someone else's hopes
broken in pieces
when the master of routine
dispossesses a minute of its time
to see mankind
falling one by one.

Victory

We won, we shout
the victory is mine/is ours
we yell, we say
we tell everyone…
but one wonders then
if the taste of victory is sour
or yet to win is sad
for I see tears running from pale eyes
and bitter lines make a frame
in victorious mouths
a triumphant face.

Mad Dreamer

I had a dream
and I wonder…
if dreams of dreamers
fully inside
make some damage,
do some harm
to innocent victims
of my lust.

I had a dream
and I wonder…
if taking you too deep into my heart
I drove you away from happiness,
and crossed your road
and made you sad…

I had a dream
– mad dreamer that I am –
dreaming of someone
being great,
being high
in the place
that we possess
in the land
of no man's land.

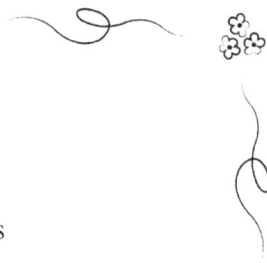

I had a dream
– endless dreamer
in my mind –
loving to the fullness
no one knows:
no unity of time,
no measure for love…

I had a dream
– ambitious dreamer I was born –
but I wonder
if I went too fast
and let my love
behind my dream,
if I made him cry
for I loved too much
and I cried as well…

The Black Has Come Back

I am sad
for I saw the world
blooming in summer
and when autumn came
I saw the leaves fall
one by one;

I am sad
for one day I felt
the climax of delight
when I found a mate,
when I found my man,
but the darkness of my eyes
covered the colours of the sun;
when a lost word
fits into its place
and filled the gap
in the puzzle of my mind.

I am sad
for I said: "yes, I trust"
but my faith
had gone far.

I am sad
for I don't hear
echoes of my prayers
and I don't recall yet
words I once said
for I don't feel
the warmth one day I felt.

I am sad
and the shades of my life
have gone fade:
the black has come back.

Miming Away the Past of Me

Miming away the past of me
I once how been
I have run into you;
I lost my head.
why were you there
if looked nowhere.
why told your lies
if I searched for minds
why flew you high
if I was on to you
if all the highlights
if you was all –
I wasted a world;
leave me alone
now
and forever
the truth was up
when the sun began to warm
and you looked at the sky
with a failure in your eyes.
forget me all;
forgive me at once
and perhaps
the me get lost;
the loss of mine
let me go
back

to what once I was
and once at all
let me alone:
your present don't share
your future and forget.

Release

Giving away the part of me
I once have been
I have run into you:
I lost my head.

Why were you there
when I went nowhere;
why told you lies
when I searched for true minds;
why flew you high
when I was on top
of all the heights
– if I was all –
I wasted a world.

Leave me alone
now
and forever.

The truth was up
when the sun began to warm
when you looked at the sky
with a failure in your eyes.

Forget me all;
forgive me at once
and release
the me yet lost;
the self of mine;
let me go
to what I have been
and once for all
let me alone:
Your present I don't share,
your future I forgot.

Becoming Quiet

Becoming quiet:
You – the wild –
Has now obeyed.
You – the rebel
Has joined the leads
To go in mass
One by one
And after the third
To the same end,
Yet unknown
But promises, thy say.
You – the wise
Have asked for help
And given back
Advise for me advice
You – the great –
Hasn't become diminished
By invisible effort in yonder guilt.
You – the nourishing face
Passing some transient god
How stop and sat
Longing hands –
Falling hair
On eyes now shut
BUT
You – the lonely –
Have become lonelier
The empty space
Is all you possess:

You preach and pray:
I was the only one there
But now, and again
If you don't mind –
And if I do not imitate
Could I possibly have
My piece of threat back
And... my beloved friend?

Shades

I wonder if tomorrow
– day in light; night in shadow –
will hide whispers of the unknown
linking loves,
joining hands
to decide;
to reprieve
the blue skies
I once have seen,
and make them dark
as today they dress in white;
as other time
they worn plain black.

Blinking flashes,
don't let me down
for today
I wear red,
and tonight
I will wear my soul.

Watching Life Not Passing By

If at last as now I am
I will remain
and just as today
my life will stay
I would touch
the red of dusts
and throw it inside my eyes
to draw the curtain of my sight
and see just that:
what is inside
the curtain frame
yet moved by the silence of a blind
seeing much/seeing less,
watching men
to fall and rise
watching life
not passing by.

You and I

You and I
pain and match
single thing
being twice
and unique:
you, the dream
I, the mind
battle to be won
by two; never by one
yet avoiding to be touched.
you and I:
time passed us
and didn't stop
you, the wind
I, the love
flying words
from mouth to ear
carrying ideas,
full of lust
you, the man
I, your ghost.

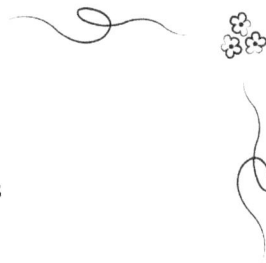

Secret Game

Colourful mornings
of a spring
ready to be summer
and a sun warming a wish,
keeping a need yet expressed
of a promise in the air
and the turning night,
in our hands:

Two beings being there and at once
no past; no future –
the "now" as a creed
and "no questions" as a rule
and time stops forever
to grab minutes in each mind
and drink the juice of lust.

A secret game
for both our brains;
a mysterious taste
for bodies used to life.

I Wonder if Tomorrow

I wonder if tomorrow
– day in light; night in shadows –
will hide whispers of the unknown
touching him
joining hand
to decide;
to enjoy
the blue skies
I once have seen
I make them dark
as today they were in white;
as other time
they were pitch black.
Thinking flashes
don't let me down
for today
I wear me and
tonight I wear my soul.
If at last as now I am
I'll remain
and just as today
my life will be portrait
I would touch
the net of dust
and throw it inside my eyes
to know the curtain of my sight
and see just that:
what is drawn
by the curtain

and just moved
by the silence
of a thing
seeing much/seeing him
watching new
to fall and rise
watching life
not passing by.

Defeated

Becoming quite:
You – 'the wild' –
has now obeyed.

You – 'the rebel' –
has joined the leads
to go in mass
and one by one
after a third
to the same end,
yet unknown,
but promised, they say.

You – 'the wise' –
have asked for help
and given back
advice for once advice.

You – 'the great' –
have become diminished
to an invisible spot
in a starless night.

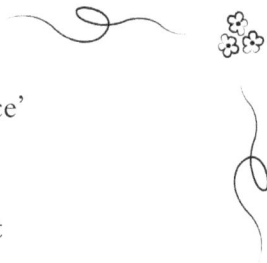

You – 'the moving face'
        'passing soul'
        'transient gal'
have stopped and sat
   – hanging hands –
   – falling hair –
on eyes yet shut;
        BUT
You – the 'lonely' –
have become lonelier;
the empty space where once were forms
        is all you possess:
You preach and pray
"I was the only one there
and I saw no one else".

Ambiguity

And all this...
the room and seats;
the books and lights;
the colourful portraits
talking of men;
speaking of me,
and hidden thoughts
now showing words
yet saying none
of my true need.

And all this,
after all,
for how long
I could keep
if empty I feel,
if I am bored
to the spleen
and soon I will leave
to start again
perhaps
in a remote spot
of this ever too small world;
perhaps not far
from this unfolded land.

Wishing to depart,
yet crying to stay:
ambiguity in fact
which only began
the day someone
pronounced a no
to something I did not ask for.

If One Day

If one day
someone would come
and say:

You – the gay –
are now to cry;

You – the singing bird –
are to stop your song
and fly away to other trees
lost in the jungle of the mist;

You – the love –
are now to hate…

If one day
someone would come
and demand
please go away
and leave us to our fate:

– your laugh annoys –
– your songs cause grief –
– your thoughts are deep –
– your lust unknown for our race –
– your dreams impossible to achieve… –

I will turn my face upward
to the clearest starts
and I will think:

It is only me
talking to myself
it is me who asks
to go away;
it is me who knows
my love has reached
the limitless lines;
is me who is gone
but to a jungle in my soul
is me who sings to life and death.
I will not go away
for never I have come
if no one every heard yet
my deepest song;
if no one every felt
the misery of my lust;
if no one ever said
please stay with us…

With Your Arms

And yet your eyes
– lusting bits of lust inside –
saying none
of what I heard
with your words;
to link one form
to a shape
still unknown
in an unbreakable embrace
meaningless to the world.

Don't talk again:
please, say 'hello'
with your lips
but say 'goodbye'
just with your arms!

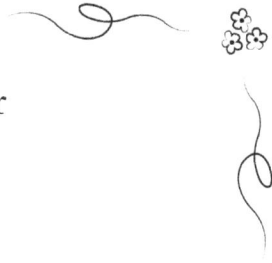

Today's Despair

Today's despair
tomorrows songs
blow to the air
by someone else.

Secrets exposed
to passing souls;
you must learn the message
and never repeat.

A question still hanging;
an answer never heard:
are yesterday's dreams
today's pain?

Memory is God

Colourful portraits
of man's despair
visual crystals
of dreams that broke
and a hand in the air
waving 'good-bye'.

The grievous knife
of an image
moving away
losing consistency,
disappearing forms,
tomorrow's legendary songs.

And the master of routine
seeing all
from the outside
and a tear strangled by a sob
– perhaps he is sad –
perhaps he laughs
and cries for it;
but hands waving no longer wave;
the light is gone
in the grey horizon
of the unknown.

Memory is powerful
– memory is god –
if there is still a chance
to forget today's despair.

Weeping

Weeps in a deserted room;
weeps in streets;
weeps anywhere
and then plain silence
as the blackout of sound
when forbidden is the dance.

Ringing bells
on a wet face
cheer up in joy:
yesterday's pain
are empty memories in your brain.

Fill them up
with cold/ice water
and drink it up
'till you see the bottom
and find yourselves
the empty space:
that is all they left.

Interference

Wishing words,
sweet and deep,
disturbing bits;
distorted pieces of thought
saturated with lust
and a whistling song
carried far out by the dins;
a nostalgic little elf
caressing the waves of sound...
I wish/I want/I need!!!
no echo to repeat
no answer to link
the distance in between;
message/no reply
and someone in the way
licking up the sweetness
and keeping the words
just for himself.

Now

"Now", we pray,
knowing well
is yet eternity in bits
reaching a name
in a nameless micro-world.

Now, simple game:
– no days before to forget;
no plans to make –
and still the echo will remain:

It was there and just once
we saw life
in our hands.

Leaving gazelle,
flying swallow,
swimming ducks,

and a nostalgic elf that repeats:
NOW.

Unfaithfulness

You come always in the night
and talk of love
to someone
who felt all shades of lust
yet felt not such.

You come to me
and close the window on the past
and draw the curtain on the world;
a line is set
around the dream:
no light to go in,
no darkness is to escape,
and two beings wait outside.
the inconsistent image of ourselves
and yet making us blind,
dream of gods;
our shelter is silent love
poor human beings playing to love!

One Wish

Words flying in the wind,
a ray of sun
to warm the bodies
yet full of life
but let alone
some winter night.

A meeting in the outside,
beyond the need
to see each one;
beneath the lust,
along the green
of a greener day:

A meeting place
in the secret joy
of beings being twice
and unique.

– Two minds –
– two bodies –
– two days –

– One wish –:
YOU AND I.

Geometry Proved Vain

And suddenly we saw
each other's face;
through a misty dream
we have been
day by day
building castles in the air,
BUT
then and at once
we saw each other
as we were:

Trembling beings;
dubious men

And face to face
knowing yet
the dreams were gone
the instant we both
looked into a mirror
and the image broke.

You – the man –
through days of lust
going back
to the start
standing alone
in the invisible line
between being yourself
or yet to belong.

I – at last –
trying to forget
and playing to be no one
with new beliefs.

I went your way
some time ago.
you walked straight
through where I now stand.

We two – the same –
standing in the air
yet saying "no";
or linking bits...:
I won't go back
what now you are
I once have been.

You won't come to me:
what now I live
you once have seen
and walked by.

A second chance
drawn for us:
you won't repent;
I won't change my mind.
we are bound to pass
and say goodbye,
or stand forever
in that line:

You, the end,
and I, the start.
geometry proved vain
when two single points
could not be joined
at once.

For Once/No More

If tomorrow,
– question mark drawn in my mind –
you, my man,
will say goodbye.

If tomorrow
– blank filled up
by the unknown –
you, my beloved,
will leave me alone.

If tomorrow
– as today I am I will be –
and beyond the sear
I will have to send my love.

If tomorrow
– empty space;
empty life –
you and I
will depart
and other eyes
will see your eyes;
and extrange arms
with hold mine,
I will pray
the master of routine:
let me be the wind
that flies;

let me go
the way I came;
let me stay
inside myself;
let me see
– for once/no more –
he who I loved;
he who I kissed
when the sun
used to melt the ice
and the light
a new colour
with my wishes built up.

When Ashes Fly

When all those we met
have gone
one by one;
when all we had
has vanished in the air
and ashes start to fly
where before there were shapes;
and ashes are only left
where one day
there were forms
and the wetness of rainfall
is missed up
with tears and sobs;
when the silence
of a night
becomes the god
and the light fades
behind the curtain of our minds,
and the earth gets cols,
and the desert need for water
matches yet
the dryness of one heart...

You, who saw
and felt
and cried;

136

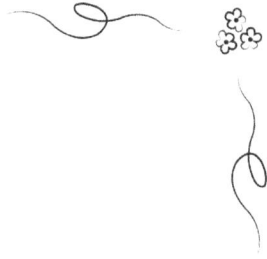

You, who knew
and failed
and climbed.

You, my friend,
don't give up.
You must last
'till the end!
knowing well
there is not much to be felt;
knowing yet we were brave.

Just to be…
be yourself.
No question to formulate
when the answers once were drawn
in the skies
long before time began
beyond man's reach.

Just forget;
just forgive;
just remain
and try "to last", please my mate…

It is Me Who is Back

When the sun fades
giving room to a misty grey,
and a plane
crosses the sky
from a summer day
to a summer night;

When a waving hand
lifts in the air
and lids cover some eyes
that shine and gloom
and hide a unity of despair;

When a room
empty before
is now filled up
by the absence of someone
side by side
with a still-alive gentle touch
and along with a book-stand;

When a sound
of music played
has no echoes
and the words
project no voice
and a curtain moves
in a window
and a lamp
is turned on,
it is me, my love,
who is back
in my room.

It is me, my man,
who is now alone
for you are far.

May I Go?

Simple statement,
"May I go"
when there are no locks
and the door is free to walk
and a whisper to deny
what loving nights
of minute-love
have built up.

Eternity forced to join
two equidistant points
in a blown word
has started its voyage.

Futility of time
banality of words
inconsistence of life.
dreaming of gods
but holding hands
with mediocrity in full.

A cold breeze
will forever blow
a place once missed
word/hidden thought
has come alive.

Impatience

If only I could
grab my life
with my two hands,
and shape it to my taste
and mould it
as I want
if only I could
hold the time
and stop the clock
or squeeze the hours
into diminutive seconds...
if only I could
place circumstance
against circumstance,
condition against condition,
man *against* man...
I, impatient thing,
could rest in peace
a shape here;
a thing beyond;
an hour there;
a time full of ideas
of my own;
a life in stares and more,
no time to wait
for time to come,
it's *NOW* and at *once:*
I want no other,
I take none else!

If the Rain

If the rain
suddenly covers the plains
and your legs
feel yet the mud
of the streets.

If the night is dark
for all the starts
forgot to shine;
you close your curtain
and produce
your individual light;

And day after day
the negative aspect of yourself
goes closing windows
slamming doors,
lighting lamps;
be sure
you don't lock
the doors of
your heart
I close forever
a chance
of seeing the world
the way it was
forever will remain.

don't try in vain
there is no choice...
of sun, or DARK!

If the wind opens your window
and moves the curtain
in a waving oscillation
you rush to slam it
and be sure
it doesn't open again;
if the sea wets your face
in unexpected rise
beyond the limit you feared
you jump and get away
to safer sands…

Tears in My Soul

Containing a distant noise,
overwhelmed with tears
some eyes getting close
and a soul
that heard much pain
but showed none;
echoes of a salutation
that kept the bitter taste
of someone gone,
while some what lips
could only get dry
often saying
is you who I want
but saying goodbye…

Waiting

Wait and wait
'till I come and go.
perhaps 'till he comes.
"from-to to-from"
– psychology of no hope -
No…
I wait for no one
I wait just a chance
layers of expectations
constitute my life.
amalgamation of seconds in a hand
while the other waves good-bye
procrastination is my fate
I wait again
– tomorrow –
the sun might rise up
and the morn
would show the unknown face
in the silence of the night
the beating of a heart
– no noise would camouflage
the knock-knock of chance –
waiting 'till waiting
can be done alone
– no one would come –
– no one would go –
the minutes have grown
inside and burn
the inside of my heart

to the unending hours
yet becoming gods.
who is there?..
and when?
The moribund noise of hope
spoke.
and the ghost of a mythical time
replied:
"Is me who is gone"
– no one else has come –
the questions she used to make
and the anguish
reflected in the face.
the why and no
symbolic revolt
of someone with brains.
Shouldn't you vanish in the air
– so, in this world
there is no place
for pretty girls
who think a lot.
go away.
They try to destroy
yet alienate
your thoughts/your life
and what you are now
is all they want
but for themselves
run away and pass on
to the jingles of the unknown.
Let the world

know nothing of your violence
and those who you met
would say
she was here one day
the next... she was not.

Sparkling Eyes

Sparkling eyes:
a game of light,
orgiastic clarity
of legendary gods.
is that the sun
yet setting down,
or else, is gold
plain in your mouth,
straight in your palate...

The dreaming of silver days,
of the thinking of now
refusing that all
when younger
pronounced a "no".

The light I saw
once in our lives
when face to face
I tasted freedom,
that was my goal.
I dream of that
– no silver, no crystals –
– no penthouse or palace –
I, with the sun, and you, my love!

Ten Past

Ten past.
the train yet goes.
the plane just came.
roads of parallel lanes
going straight,
opposite direction,
don't touch,
don't reach,
but say good bye
before diversion.
a black spot has set in front.
to overtake just seems the law
who dared had
the black I never had
to get it now
no time to wait –
reaching the end
who saw the men
that crossed the road,
who felt the rain
that fell and refreshed
the sweating foreheads,
and the echoes reclaims
some nice/sweet words
once yet pronounced/implored/and forgot…

Pain

Pain,
deep down your soul
and a cold mind
to see life
– no matter what –
fights its way
against destiny
destroying your being,
the ashes built from ashes
remaining yet
you were no one
fought against destruction
and, as ever,
lost.

God,
from beginning to end
across your brains
to realise
despite of all –
the pity, the justice, the good
are dead, all in one
while your swore not to procrastinate,
never to resign.

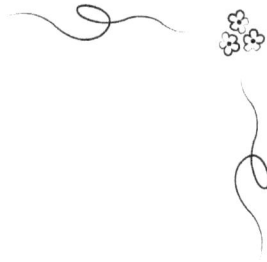

Life

Life,
intangible threat
around one's neck,
burning substance
and solid pain
– tangible for once –
when life might faint.

I

I,
a little girl,
yet more belittled
by the wild world.

I,
the great loneliness,
pen in hand,
and a glass of wine
running off liquid,
running off money
it is before pay-day.

I,
the goddess,
not a joint to smoke,
not a brain to hare my pains,
and the sun
– for once –
(winter is here to stay)
heating up my artificial hair –

Today,
the greatest I ever met
is empty,
is sad,
is lonely,
is broke
and has not even got
a joint to smoke.

Alone

Alone,
you go through life
fate following your steps
no one holding your hand
and your shadow like yourself
is left behind
where lights go by.

Lonesome roads
for your pace,
speeding thoughts
of people gone
and waving hands
not risen yet
yet sweating good-by.

They came
they left.
transient shadows
in grey skies
wind flying north
rain falling down
not living souls
to share a thought.

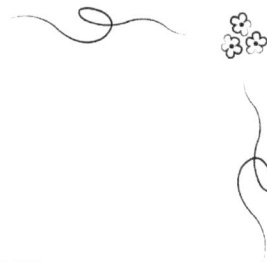

Wandering

Wandering being
step in front of step
sometimes beyond the seas
and always looking ahead
forgetting or not remembering
the acquired friend.

Bits of still life
gathered from shore to land
one day unknown
today well in the past
but never quite gone
lingering souls
that came and went
souvenirs that stayed
impregnated with desire
now hanging from the walls.

Where are you my friends
the words we spoke
the whispers of love
feelings we felt
ideas exchanged
profound thoughts.

You came and went
or I walked away
wandering soul
today I am alone.

Cosmic Dust

Lonely Nomad in no man's land
casting shadows on virgin sands
ethereal clouds
with inner light
no roots to set
no marks to leave
uttering no sound in their despair
and not a trace
when sun sets down
visions that begun
when man wasn't man
and cosmos was just dust.

Transient beings
passers-by from alien lands
and seas in between
now reaching shores
steamed by the sun
and shedding futile lives
that became their past
silhouettes that have seen
the verge of lust
and conquered death.

Dispersed particles in perennial search
mirages on deserts sands
cosmic rays
time has come to reunite
and forever project
two shadows into one.

Has Left No Trace

Rain forever wets the fields
rivers will join the seas
and clouds will form and dissipate
but love, love comes and stays.

Scratch the inner self
of he who once has loved
and love will pour out
the tears once shed
without pain now,
without a sound.

Years came and went
memories and faces were around
but he who loved
has love inside
and love stays
perennial pain.

Where have all lovers gone
when at sunset
the carcass of the heart
has been worn out
'cause love, love stayed,
but the beloved
has left no trace.

From the Outside

From the outside
looking at oneself,
they joy of being alive
while words are never said,
no future, no past tense,
only today's desires
and the lingering wish
for yet a longer day.

One more time,
just once, why not more,
perhaps tomorrow, maybe today,
but knowing too well
feelings are doomed to fade
although in two minds
memories will forever remain
for we cast shadows
in deserted sands
and instead of two projected one.

Transient Beings

Transient beings
in perennial search,
today by the sea,
but watching the waves
and wanting to leave.

Ethereal souls
from alien worlds,
perceptive brains
without a friend,
walking alone
the paths of life,
anguish in their thoughts,
eyes lit up with fire.
soon they will be gone
when the wind blows
and the question will remain,
who were they who came
when the tide was high;
who were they who felt
the joys of desire,
and cried when they left,
wasted tears in arid lands,
while uttering goodbye.

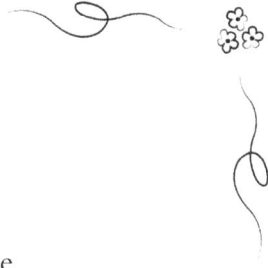

Stalemate

Stalemate,
robots of mankind
assembled in one place,
the purpose the same,
motionless puppets
manipulated at wish,
humanoid beings
who became misfits.
effigies of the human race,
now outcasts,
while I – the iconoclast –
rebel.

Life Walker

Life walker
of quiet moves,
and secret ways,
and sensuous lips,
around the world
in search for love,
stay a while
the day has gone,
remain in silence,
set time adrift.

Passenger of time,
collecting thoughts
from shore to land.
unspoken words
that once were loud
but now are quiet,
remain nearby
a longer day.

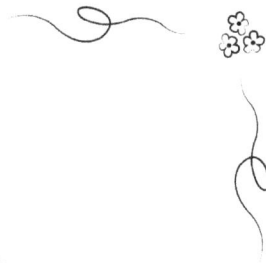

Bohemian being
of golden skin
kissed by the sun
in foreign lands,
the impetus of youth
is your mirage,
for there is no love,
but loveful moments;
for there is no land
but sea-less shores;
for there is no truth
but there is silence
in nomad sands.

Bits of Still Life

Bits of still life
in suspended animation
that a short spin of time
broke away from lassitude
as they left deep impassions.
moments that took shape
to become unforgetful.
volatile as the wind,
transient mood
that soon fades
and no sorrow,
or regret,
or tomorrow
will exist.
just the price
of grabbing life
with both hands,
while it lasts;
just the taste
of having lives
to the climax of oneself.

Don't Get Too Close

"Don't get too close"...
The echo of said words
lingers in the air,
remembrance of love
wanting to remain,
yet wishing to fade.
Ambivalence portraying
the needs of yesterday,
the newly found self.
complex wanderer
of mysterious strength
open your soul
and don't be afraid
for I won't complain;
for no one will know;
for I won't behold;
for soon I will be gone
the way I came
and you, once again,
will search and forget
while I will remember
the moments of love
then hidden forever,
then painfully lost.

The Pleasures of the Flesh

The pleasures of the flesh
leave behind immense pain;
the pleasures of the mind
give great anguish
to the soul.
What is left
in the human world
to commit oneself
if man betrays man,
the scarcest hours,
the link to life.
Man is vain.
Pleasure is futile.
transient distress
I recognize your face;
this time go away
once and for all
as I surrender
my need for joy,
my thirst forever.

Freedom

Freedom as my goal,
freedom as my creed,
let me be myself
in spontaneity
as I wish to be.
freedom to love,
freedom to pronounce
the whispering sounds
that ecstasies gives,
unselfish state
without false pretence,
without a farce,
no questions asked,
no need to explain
when the body claims
some restful time;
or when the mind has gone ahead
to dreamers' land
other wishes to fulfil;
or as today
you have no need for me;
let freedom be
the reason not to lie
as deeply it hurts
to love someone
in freedom's sake
while truth is alien.

Yours is Silence

Feelings
of overwhelming strength,
deep and profound
yet hidden.
Words
strangled sounds,
uttered and restrained.
thoughts
of strange depth
and all forbidden.
wishes
through the frontiers
of the allowed,
beyond the unknown,
perennial meaning
the force of time
could never fade
and all in one
must remain as it was
as fears not expressed
have proclaimed
two stand points, two ways.
misunderstood need;
uncomprehended words
overwhelmingly deep
and alien to your peace
the inner peace
set now on trial.
I am passing through

and superficial marks
is all I left
though words could have explained
I have remained quiet;
intensity is my name,
but yours is silence.

The Longest Hour

The longest hour
that time when anxiety sets in
and the body conquers
the mind's best will.
awaiting in silence
aware and alert
to incoming sounds,
perceptive state
but at the end
pain and distress
the time has flown by,
depression reigns,
darker nights after the splendour,
emptier lives,
the vacuum of time
has come and gone
leaving man behind.

Anguish of Today

Anguish of today,
feelings eroding the soul,
are you not the same
of some years ago.

Multicolour rainbows
in skies deep blue,
glittering lights,
of transient truth
and longer lasting shadows,
hide the simmer
that deceitfully attracts,
for man is naive,
for man will never learn
sincerity is a myth
and love does not exist.
Reality is a ghost
that floats around the world
and self is never one
but a perennial two,
ambivalent portrait
of simultaneous beings,
to smile and yet to cry
both at the same time,
O man, give up the trial,
O man, capitulate.

Floating Cloud

Floating cloud
holding on
at the mercy of desert winds,
purposeless and lost,
without a link
to man or cause,
aimlessly moving
towards no end,
the move itself being the goal.

Marionette of time,
drifting desire
in someone's hands,
awaiting in silence
and quiet sobs
no one can hear
and secret tears
no one can see
disrupt the peace,
while deeper anguish
is settling in,
while painful dreams
are nesting in.

Those nameless games
with secret scores,
then without shadows,
now without light
must now be named.
name too the blunder
to reach the soul,
and name the failure
to share the thought,
distorted feelings
while holding on
reflections in the sky
have become shadows in the day.

Withdrawal Time

Withdrawal time,
the self within the self,
secret parade to oblivion,
silent shadows in the horizon
marching alone,
soundless move to solitude.

Unspoken words,
feelings led to exile
before they were born.
phantoms in the night,
strangling the soul,
seclusion of the mind
expressionless facade
with yet a smile
the truth now in disguise.

Gone before they came,
untouched and unfulfilled,
a distant paradise
too far to reach
but no one knew then
and no one will ever know
for written words
are secretly kept
and forbidden thoughts
are to be extinct,
the link to man
was a mirage
in golden sands
the wind brought rain.

Why

And why, and why
accosts the mind

Reasons to explain,
causes to justify
the change of heart

While knowing well
yet from the start
there was no future
but there was end
and futile feelings
backed by no meaning
were doomed to fade.

The day has come
though knowing fate
the soul has entered
a limbo of time.
no longer days,
no silent smiles,
no secret joy
no sounds to utter,
no one to share
the glint of love,
though very transient,
though very vain
and very quiet
inside itself

the mind has prayed
for one to explain
and kiss farewell
at least for once
when mind and body
and soul and hope
will then surrender
and drift away
to distant lands
without a word
without a sound.

Like a Ghost

Like a ghost
a silent shadow passing through
you come and go.
Soundless moves
yet a turmoil
is deep inside the mind and soul,
to need and not to wish
to express the need.
to want and yet to choose
not to have.
To know the road
and yet to keep a low profile
while days go by
and nights arrive.
strange being,
wanderer in solitude,
your life's desires
mixed and confused.
If only one could stretch ones hands
and quietly your thirst relieve.
if only one could gently touch
your inner self,
the hidden anguish
and sooth and calm
pain and distress.
but you remain aloof
and you remain silent.
your needs are all profane,
my hands are tied…

Alone I Stand

Alone I stand,
detached and uncommitted
to mankind and their world.
Solitude is my choice,
silent hours of deep thoughts
meditating or remembering,
or just lasting,
inking perhaps both
the reality and the dream.
Trust rests upon no one
and no one will fail again.
no pain will emanate
from their game
on human farce.
no transient lights
will brighten days
to go sombre at sunset
when the glimmer
slowly fades
and the shadows become silhouettes.
I stand alone
from now and no,
detached and unfulfilled,
knowing well what not to wish
but ignoring what to want.
drifting life of a bohemian,
lonely soul in search no longer
for the world was found small
for mankind and myself.

Like Graffiti

Like graffiti
engraved on sand,
semi-circles and crossing lines,
drawn by words
of futile meaning,
and low voices,
and silent smiles
in the desert summer nights.
amorphous shapes
now concealing casted shadows
Fused in one.
tangled feelings,
crossing fates,
then approaching
golden sunsets,
now marching parallel.
split reflections,
aberrations
of passions lost
when reality cut across
their secret paths.
Lonely silhouettes
marching away,
setting distance in between
and who never
will meet again.
marionettes
in someone's game,
though graffiti

is now drawn up
on the shores
of Arabian seas
where the waves
its shape will banish
on my heart
where it will languish.

Today I Lost

Sometimes your name
breaks through oblivion walls,
jumps seclusion boundaries
to happily parade
in front of me.
I struggle and fight
the thought, the need
and close my eyes
so not to see
a flying kiss
that has just threatened
my lips to leave.
sometimes you win
and I succumb
and delve into the past,
sweet days that went
too fast to make a mark
on anyone else
but did on me.
sometime you lose
the kiss that fled
has returned gone,
my arms controlled
will not embrace
your body's ghost;
the need to speak,
the anguish felt
will hide away.
but then, perhaps,

the day will come
when both at once
will call a truce
to win and lose
both at the same time
and with hands fused
will walk away
to greener lands
for one more dream
for one more pain.
today, I lost.

Living Life

Living life in short spasms,
one day at a time
but no more than on.
letting passions thrive
and desires be born,
and remaining alert
to the human sounds
now being expressed,
but never pronounced.

Distorted view
across a facade
that excluded the inner truth.
the needs of one day
– and a day at a time –
are memories forged
in Arabian nights
when silence spread
and dreams were let out.
for better a dream
to remain unattained
perennial illusion
or eternal meaning
unforgettably strong –
than the taste of solitude
left behind
when wandering feelings
confront reality and say farewell
to become the past tense.

Passenger of Time

Passenger of time
cruising through life
aloof and detached
and closed to no one
remaining somewhere
a day or a night
departing again
when day breaks
and night darkens.

Why turn back your head
if farewell was long said.

Why glance in the past
shadows fading,
empty spaces.

Why prolong the moments of silence,
lingering silhouettes
when it is time for sunset.

Why slow down the pace
if your march long commenced
the time you kept quiet,
the hour when love fled.

Mirror Image

Mirror image,
when a smile reflects a smile,
and gentle sobs echo more sobs
and when silence
remains more silence.

I am the face
behind the glass
that cries and laughs
when pain and joy
are felt on earth.

And I am love
if love is given
but I turn cold
to hidden feelings.
and I am desire
if you are in flames,
the entire range
of passions felt
will be displayed.
and if at night,
when facades drop,
the rougher corners
of hassling days
then in disguise
still remain,
I will be stone
to sharpen them

and I will be hurt
but you won't know.
and if at sunset
when sounds die off
and turbid waters
reflect the moon,
a secret need,
a thirst for truth,
a touch then soft,
I will be the fountain
of profound peace
providing only
the deepest love
then unconcealed,
and then exposed.

Non-guilty Hands

An infinite cover of whiteness
I flashed my eyes,
gazed at me
as forgiving any sins
from other lives,
as erasing any anguish from wasted hours
in yet compromised beings;
the you in you,
my I inside
with both our right hands
touching the flower of time
for you were there
and I was besides
and double echoes of our voices
transmitted a "yes"
beyond the whiteness to no end,
to a limitless sky,
to a time that time itself can not deny,
to a blank of guilt
in non-guilty hands.

Del Amor y la Vida: Poemas de mi Juventud en Español

Solo Dios

La noche está fría, la noche está clara,
La luna no estaba, no estaba la luna,
Estaba yo solo demasiado solo,
El sauce rendía sus hojas al viento
Me paré un momento y miré las aguas,
Que sucias estaban las aguas.
En sus leves olas se veía el mundo
todas tan unidas, todas tan distantes.
¿Y por qué esas dos querían unirse?
Se amaban querían ser una que sobresaliera
¿Es que no quieren que sean felices?
Oigan esperen un poco; les dice una voz
es una voz antigua que quiere que sean como ellas
fueron.
Pero, si tenemos nosotros más vida,
si el tiempo nos muestra más pronto el amor
¿Porqué rechazarlo, es malo que nos queramos tanto?
Dejad que vivamos nuestra juventud.
Y si al fin no tenemos fuerza para seguir luchando
El Amor es nuestro Viento y contra él…
Solo Dios.

Me Querías

I

Me querías y te quería, que felices fuimos
Nuestros corazones supieron que es amar
Tú y yo vivimos lo que sentimos
Y mi alma enamorada solo quería cantar.

II

Todo iba muy bien hasta aquel día…
Aquel 15 de mayo terrible y triste,
nos separamos sinceros y con valentía
y aquella noche agria, aquí viniste.

III

Ahora el tiempo ha transcurrido un poco
tú por un sendero ajeno a mí, vas
mientras sufro y triste a Dios invoco
aprendiendo a quererte mucho… más…

IV

Tal vez eres un cobarde, tal vez un valiente
fueras lo que fueses te quiero todavía…
pero a perjudicarte, no vuelvo nuevamente
aunque me deshaga en la noche y en el día.

V

Y si de nuevo vuelves a mí algún día
Dios quiera que ese día no sea tarde
porque aquel inmenso amor que te tenía
lo mataste… por valiente o por cobarde.

Octubre

Dime Octubre, oh dime, di
por qué tienes en tu luna ahora
dos reflejos tan extraños para mí
porqué tornas a mi alma ilusiones
que febril casi me hacen ver visiones,
que acompañan a mi alma que estaba sola
Dime a mi Octubre, di
que será de otros amores que vinieron,
en que loca de amor me consumí
por las que sacrifiqué mi vanidad,
por qué las traes que volvieron
a opacar o aumentar mi felicidad
y me duele ser feliz de nuevo
porque es tarde y ya no puedo
compartir mi felicidad con el que amé.

Y hoy que te despides, mes ansiado,
queda en mi corazón un gran dolor
al saber que siento de mucho amor
pero no para un corazón que quise demasiado.

Con mi Luna Amiga

Mira la luna, qué linda! con nubes negras, negras así me
gusta más..
Todo llega a mi memoria, las noches aquellas que quedan
atrás.
Pero, mírala ahora, qué pálida está
parece que quisiera y no pudiera suspirar…
Ya pasa y esa nube no volverá;
me gusta su cara, no la he de olvidar
semeja tantas cosas, me dice muchas más
y trata de escucharme cuando le quiero hablar.

Conoce mis secretos, yo se los he contado
en noches como ésta, de poca claridad
en que nebulosa y rara ha estado
lo mismo que mi alma que quisiera llorar.

Su luz tenue me alcanza
ensaya a comprenderme, pretende consolarme
y se queda silenciosa mientras la noche avanza
y pronto es la hora de entrarme.

Hay veces que juntas lloramos,
porque la luna también llora,
nadie lo sabe pues solas siempre estamos,
la luna también mis recuerdos añora.

Ahora, mira que luz tan fuerte
que me dice, ah! Me dice soy tu amiga
conmigo si puedes vente
sin que sufras, sin intrigas.

Inmensa placidez envuelve mi alma,
me siento en una lejanía,
olvidado todo me parezco a una santa,
la miraré siempre, es amiga mía.

De mis Noches

Miro llegar las noches lentamente
y siento la proximidad de tu presencia
muy dentro de mí está latente
un recuerdo tenaz por tu ausencia,
mas espero en vano tu llegada,
un vago presentimiento toma formas,
me aprisiona las sienes una idea
y es que tú ya no retornas
porque no quieres que yo te vea
y la angustia me estremece el corazón
siento mis ojos por las lágrimas bañados
tú que fuiste y serás mi adoración
solo quieres ahora caminos separados.

Llegaban a mí, venían ligeras,
como unos rumores, como esos de ayer,
llenaban mi alma, semejaban luceros
cuya luz tan pequeña se olvidan de ser
y sentía tan dentro una profunda nostalgia
vagaban en mi mente los recuerdos
que cegando mis ojos como por magia
recordaban mis seres amados ya muertos.

Pero muertos son todos los que se han ido
Los que viven y añoro con amargura
los que amé, amé más ya el olvido
se encargó de borrarlos aún sin mi ayuda.

Más al correr el tiempo y esperar
que de una nube brotes algún día
me siento tranquila pues sé amar,
estoy casi segura que tu alma es mía.

Viniste ya tantas veces, hoy también,
felices recorrimos indiferentes calles
es un recuerdo más que ceñirá mi sien
pues te veo en mis pupilas tan lleno de detalles.

Kahio

No sé qué decías cuando apretando mis
manos con vos contenida apenas modulabas
"Ceci… Ceci… " y yo te entendía o quería hacerlo.
Tu llamado iba a mis entrañas
y me removía cuanto de sensible hay en ellas…
Kahio! Kahio.
Yo no pronuncio ya tu nombre,
ya lo he dicho tantas veces,
con llanto desgarrador
con ansias locas
con tristeza infinita
con tanto amor…
Y ya lo he gastado para mi voz.
Hube de gritarlo muchas veces
apretando mi almohada a mis labios para acallar mi
llamado
que siempre sería vano, vano…

Ahora vienes tú y me llamas aquí…
aquí a mi lado y con mis manos en las tuyas
Oh, viejo amor! Viejo muy viejo.
Que envejeció de tanto querernos en silencio
y de quererte yo sola cuando tú pretendiste olvidarme.
Oh, inmensísimo amor, amor pasado.
Perdona que no te escuche ahora
porque ya nuestros nombres he olvidado.

Te Vas

Te vas…
Tú siempre te estás yendo:
te fuiste de mí,
te vas de mi ciudad,
pero nunca te podrás ir
de mi recuerdo de ti.
a donde vayas te persigo,
sin seguirte estás conmigo.

Yo Quisiera que el Tiempo se Parara

Si yo pudiera detener el tiempo
y aprisionarlo entre mis manos frías
para conservar la felicidad que estoy sintiendo…
Si yo pudiera guardar en el alma mía
todos esos instantes que ya huyeron
un eterno presente de ilusión yo te daría.
Yo quisiera que el tiempo se parara
cuando tengo tus manos muy unidas,
y al mirar tus ojos, que el mundo no contara
para decirte en secreto lo que nunca se olvida
y recordarte en mil besos lo mucho que te amaba…
Más, debo cerrar mis ojos para guardar tu cara
porque al abrirlos de nuevo me encontraré con tu
ausencia
y un reloj que descansa en mi muñeca me recordará a
cada instante que la felicidad se va de mi vida.

Y te Llamo

Una cosa triste cuando estoy triste
es que tu nombre regresa a mis labios
y trato de creer que no existes,
de callar mi inexplicable llamamiento
pero es vano
ya he escrito tu nombre para no pronunciarlo.

Una cosa me extraña cuando me siento débil
y es que acuden a ti mis fuerzas idas
para apoyarse pues eres muy hombre,
más he de recobrar las fuerzas mías
y de callar siempre tú nombre
aunque ya lo haya escrito y ahora lo diga.

Las Oscuras Sombras de Mi Viaje Triste

Si no fuese este mi camino, no dejes, Señor, que me
pierda en el regreso.

Para que no vuelvan mis ojos al pasado,
ciega, Señor, con tu luz mis pupilas que no te verán si no a Ti
en todo lo viejo que ya he recorrido.

En las oscuras sombras de mi viaje triste,
que me ilumine siempre, Señor, la esperanza que de días
venideros se desprende.

Cuando la ausencia de un detalle colme de vacío mi
existencia,
llénalo tú con la plenitud de tu única gracia.

Más quisiera que la tenue luz relativa de mi estrella fuese
mi única fuente de energía para no revivir con la luz del
día pasado.

Dime por qué, di!
cuando encuentro silencio en su corazón,
vuelve el mío sus brazos hacía ti que te has tornado sordo!

Bañada en los días de plenitud me enfría ahora la
"saudade" de tus cosas para mí.
Ya no temo al olvido: sola sufriría y nadie reconocería mi
rostro entre la gente porque no ostentará su faz demacrada!

A Mi Pesar te Sueño

A pesar del tiempo y la distancia,
a pesar de los besos de otra boca
y del ardiente amor que me cobija,
yo sigo pensando en ti como una loca
y olvido las promesas que me brindan
para recordar hasta tu más sutil palabra.
Se abren ante mí muchos caminos
y si les doy una mirada complacida
se llena mi corazón con tu ausencia
porque te deseo compartir mi vida;
Sé que lejanísimos están nuestros destinos,
sé que hay más que una alma en tu ser;
pero yo que te quise primero y olvidarte quisiera
no logro borrar de mi cara
las huellas heladas de tus besos de ayer;
ni opacan otros ojos de intensa mirada
la profunda felicidad que me dejaste grabada;
hoy solo un eco muy distante queda de tu voz
y exprimo de tus palabras hasta la última gota de tu amor.
A mi pesar te sueño y en la noche oscura
de este largo olvido
me opacan las imágenes con vida tu irreal figura
para recordarme luego que tú me dijiste "adiós"…

Mis Ojos Claros

Yo miraba siempre al cielo
y de tanto mirar
claros mis ojos se volvieron;
yo miraba al mar
y mis ojos creyeron
que a góticas de él iban a llegar;
y si al sol estaba, miraba sus destellos
que con su brillo mis ojos hacían cerrar.
Y así llegó un día en que tuve que llorar
sentada en los rincones mis ojos quisieron
verter todo el llanto que pudieran albergar
y si eran mis ojos claros
más claros tendrían que quedar
y si parecían goticas de mar
ya serían arroyos o dos lagos.
Hoy me pregunta la gente
qué cosa extraña mis ojos tienen
Que no alcanzan a descifrar
parece alegría como de fuente
o una gran pena que quieren ocultar
y ese fulgor que llevan siempre…
y ellos no pueden contestar
que en ellos quedó latente
Un amor dormido que siempre los hará brillar.

La Aurora de Mi Soledad

En la aurora de mi último instante contigo
no temo tu partida ni el sentirte lejano de mi propio ser;
temo la bruma cegadora que empieza con faz de hastío
y que se tornará en la soledad que ya me empieza a envolver
a los gritos salvajes de nuestros lugares conocidos.

Hoy que te alejas de mí y que muchas lunas pasarán
antes de que tus brazos me vuelvan a recordar
es necesario que calles al mundo tu secreto,
es necesario que tus labios solo digan mi nombre
porque quiero persistir en tu anhelo
y las horas que quedaban ya se van…

Vete! Vete ansioso de irte y no volver.
Vete loco de dicha y de ilusiones
no importa lo que ha quedado atrás…
lucha por hacer con tu ideal un nido
que yo correré a él para quitar mi frío!

Lloré en Silencio

Anoche hubo muerte en mí dentro…
Agonizó un instante y luego… nada!
lloré en silencio…

Tú luz ya no alumbraba
y sólo yo formaba el centro
de grandes esperanzas pasadas!
Te dije: mucho de ti espero,
pero ya nada esperaba;
y en ti creo…
más en ti no confiaba!
te creía grande y aún eras pequeño…

Piensa, reflexiona sin miedo
y conócete tú mismo para que puedas construir,
para que mañana puedas dar…
pero te tuve que mentir,
ya de eso no te siento capaz…

Tuviste la dicha en tus manos y la dejaste partir
y hoy que regresas a mi dormido
veo que te atrasaste en ti mismo,
que tu yo quedo atrás
porque llevaste a un abismo
la conciencia que te hacía pensar,
y pasas tu vida callada
y yo he de hablar por los dos
y aunque tome tus manos para hacerte reaccionar
solo hay algo muy cierto:
mis manos solo te dicen adiós…
Tú, para mí, estás muerto!

Mi Corazón Regresa a Amarte

Busqué el amor que un día abandonara
en la intrincada selva de tu vida,
marché a otros lugares que yo ansiaba
poseer y fue para ti mi ida
la más dura razón que tú ignorabas.

Necesité que el tiempo transcurriera,
que muchos soles lejos de ti se me ocultaran,
que otras lunas opacasen la misma luna que mirabas.

Estar al lado de personas diferentes
que brindaron momentáneos sentimientos,
valorar las personas que no mienten
y no volver a mi pasado un pensamiento.

Hoy es ese día en que pretendo
hallar a mi corazón despedazado,
al que dejé solo casi muriendo
por la única razón de haberme amado.

Y retorno una noche muy oscura a ti
después de haber sabido en tus ojos llanto
que nunca me dolió saberlo tanto
como hoy ya no lloras más por mí
y que pienso que no dejaste ver tu sufrimiento.

Ahora vuelvo a ti, Corazón Mío
buscando mi amor, lo encuentro dormido
como se duerme un niño después de haber llorado un
rato.

Necesité verte sufrir, sola dejarte
más nunca me imaginé que tu pudieras
ser de otro, que para él vivieras
ahora que mi corazón regresa a amarte.

Volverás conmigo alguna vez,
estarás para siempre a mi lado
o ya no retornarás pues se ha olvidado
lo felices que pudimos siempre ser
por el mucho tiempo que ha pasado?

Muerte en Vida

Una muerta en vida. Cabalgante sirena de mares muy vírgenes, en potros extraños de un violáceo sueño irreal: Crecer! La montura que despedaza las amadas piernas, las muy amadas; guardadoras perennes de secretos sufridos, olvidados ya. Dolorosas estrellas que hipnotizan una mente vacía de alegrías con no menos ponzoñas que una vida. Un reflejo oscilante que a peso de brillar con sadismo logra derretir las amargas tinieblas creadas por el convencimiento; por la única certeza absoluta: la de carecer de un valor real. La de no poseer nada que dure más que una soledad.

Emerge una idea. Se acaricia un deseo y las palabras truncas por ruidos impersonales de mecanismo hastiado destruyen la reencarnación. Qué dura más el amargo de la espera sin que el acto se haya consumado. Y qué duele más el volver a morir que el morir por primera vez.

Ajeno es Mi País

Unas montañas como fin, y esperanza. No como las cercanísimas y muy altas que agotaron mi aire un día; pero, al fin y al cabo, las mismas desgraciadas! Que si una vez enrarecieron mi atmósfera, éstas sólo enmarcan el frío de una ciudad fría poblada por habitantes fríos. La impotente ceguera del que quiere mirar un más allá y tenazmente su deseo se ve obstruido por murallas irregulares, de tierra estéril, de soledad cómplice de ratas humanas, fruto imperativo de entes que a pesar de su asquerosos hacinamiento, no se unen en una sola causa y cuyas incatalogables pasiones sobrepasan el Bien y el Mal.

El constante traqueteo de un artefacto eléctrico, de fabricación extranjera es mi inmediato vecino. El mismo debería estar aporreado con el vigor de una juventud con vida, pero a un ritmo acompasado y suficientemente recio para sobrepasar al primero y hojas blancas llenas de letras yuxtapuestas formarían una idea; hasta un posible concepto. Pero ajeno. Siempre ajeno. Como lo son las horas de este día, seguido y perseguido de otros tantos… ajenos, claro está. Ajenos como las mismísimas montañas y los espacios llanos que son una sola pretensión de horizonte y que desertan de su ambición al inmediato contacto de un montón de tierra para consolarse con un ángulo geométrico.

continúa

Ajeno es mi país. Paradójica secuencia expresada desde un alma sola y desolada. Pintorescas visiones que por el derecho de natura les corresponde representar las manos del que muchas veces aporreó sus carnes para sacar los alimentos húmedos de llanto, ennegrecidos por un sudor de esfuerzo sin justa ocasión de limpieza.

Ajena es la ciudad. Lugar impermisible para el que loco de propia angustia busca ahogarla en los horrendos ruidos de mecánica reparada y bocinazos enfurecidos, onomatopeyas de palabras impronunciables que demasiado frecuentemente toman expresión oral, turbando así a los que, para su desgracia aún tienen Fé.

Ajeno el parque público. Burla sagaz de un grupo autoritario que guarda para sí hasta el verde de los prados en reservados terrenos rebanados del cuerpo de estáticos edificios, copia fiel de otros muchos levantados hace muchos vanos años y en lugares lejanos, y repetidos tantas veces como el miserable jura y perjura de su vida.

Ajeno mi país. Mis paisajes, Mis parques y ciudades. Ajena es mi vida en sus 15 horas de luz; precio establecido sobre mi imponente cuerpo de bebé con la necesidad de comer por testigo.

Hoy que siento las manecillas del reloj como puñales en las entrañas mismas de mi enfermizo deseo de vivir, de pensar y poseer!, el 12 del mediodía que determina mi libertad mental se me hace inalcanzable, lejano y profanado. He de doblegar mi capacidad de formar ideas; he de vencer y esconder mi deseo de alejarme. No se ha creado un sitio para mí, si mi propio país es ajeno.

Always, During My Lifetime

Era como un caballo, un caballo negro y muy salvaje;
amaba el sol, la lluvia.
Se extasiaba sintiendo el tirón de su crin al engarzarse en
los enmarañados follajes y jugaba a los gnomos con los
divertidos rayos de sol que se filtraban por las ramas… y
corría… corría con ansias locas de llegar al infinito, como
puede hacerlo un fanático y a velocidad de las nubes en
tormenta. La oscuridad de la noche excitaba sus sentidos;
era mayor el ansia de sentir, de oler, de estar vivo y
sentirse dueño de su vida.

Y llegó un día el hombre… parecía tan solo… y juraba
amistad.
Ya no importaba el dirigir sus ansias hacia otros lados
porque coincidía con las ansias de otro ser… de un
"humano"! y el placer de compartir era aún mayor, y la
presencia del hombre añadía un no-se-qué de extraño y
excitante… algo que nunca antes – ni aún dentro de su
increíble y único mundo! – había conocido. Y pasaban las
horas – eran quizás centurias – pero nada parecía minar
la excitación.

Más llegó otro día en que, sin dar tiempo a expresión de sentimientos, el hombre partió. Y eran entonces la selva más tupida.

La noche más oscura;

y las nubes jamás se dejaron ganar en su carrera.

El verde era oscilante y el agua sabía a lodo. Y así pasó mucho más tiempo – quizás solo fueron horas! – y el negro que había en su dentro; que siempre estaba adherido a su mismísima piel, se cubrió de coraje y valor. Se sabía dueño de un tesoro que nadie poseía y ya no lo compartiría jamás! Y sirvió su negrura de coraza protectora y fue así como otro día quiso el hombre volver, hastiado de su propio egoísmo! El brío que manaba de su fuerte contextura parecía derretirse y se sintió desfallecer. Quiso huir y sacudió su crin al viento, ahora más fuerte que jamás! – pero ese mismo viento le llevaba los gritos angustiados del que antes juró amistad. Volvió sus pasos hacia él…. Aproximándose lentamente, con automatismo – hecho inaudito en algo que es todo "vida" y "movimiento"! – pero miró su cara y lo sintió inferior.

Always Myself to Myself

No sufras por amor! Deja que te quieran muchos. Que te conozcan y admiren; compréndelos tú, tenles afecto y estimúlalos para que progresen, para que sean hombres, para que triunfen… pero tú… no sufras porque ellos se puedan ir de ti, solo ir porque a ti no te olvidan del todo, tú dejas huella en ellos , tú modificas sus rumbos y ningún cambio se echa al olvido. Y mientras… conoce, conoce a más, no te aferres a uno, a alguien con miedo de perderlo. Tú vales mucho y más valor hay en ti cuando se te conoce, cuando se te diferencia y se capta hasta el más recóndito de tus actos.

Sigue adelante! Tu vida va por el camino del triunfo y serás admirada y amada pero tú… no te aferres con miedo a alguien que vendrán muchas detrás y serán superiores a medida que tú te hagas superior y hay tiempo para esperar; olvida esa carrera contra reloj que la sociedad se ha empeñado en correr. Bien sabes, y más que nadie, las ventajas de esperar… siempre esperar… y en estos asuntos el tiempo es formación y sabiduría que se te da por días y por número de personas que conozcas, que ames, que te admiren. Y mañana, tal vez tu vida se anide en un lejano y desconocido lugar que tu ignoras, que tu inconscientemente anhelas… pero no te aferres a alguien con temor de perderte; tú sabes que la monotonía solo engendra monotonía y… por qué no aventurarse, cambiar para ver los resultados; y sé prudente como has tratado de serlo siempre pero no sufras por amor ni te aferres a alguien con temor de perderle.

Hijo

Labra tu vida como ese mármol griego
donde el triunfo armonioso de la línea perdura
la vida no es tan mala cuando en su entraña dura
el optimismo enciende de la belleza el fuego;

Arde por ti la lámpara perenne de mi ruego
por ti germinan líneas sobre mi arcilla oscura
y para el tedio grave de mi hora futura
ha de ser serio estímulo esta fé que te entrego.

Que sean en tu vida meta de luz mis sueños
que las crueles aristas de los odios pequeños
y las luchas sin gloria te hagan sereno y fuerte
y cuando seas hombre, si no estoy a tu lado,
la alegría suprema de verte modelado
me llenará de rosas el yelmo de la muerte.

Index of Titles

English Titles

Spanish Titles

www.ingramcontent.com/pod-product-compliance
Lightning Source LLC
Chambersburg PA
CBHW020452100426
42813CB00031B/3341/J